Sea Creatures and Their Underwater Problems

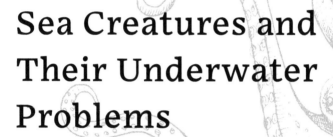

Sea Creatures and Their Underwater Problems

Viktoria Makarenko

PALMETTO
P U B L I S H I N G
Charleston, SC
www.PalmettoPublishing.com

Paperback ISBN: 979-8-8229-5042-9

This book is dedicated to:

*My beautiful parents, who always encouraged me
to chase my dreams, to feel my emotions through
and through, to unapologetically be myself and say
whatever is on my mind. Mom and dad, thank you for
never giving up on me, you raised me to be the woman
I am today, and this book would have never happened
if you didn't support me every step of the way.
I love you.*

*And my wonderful brother, my best friend.
My shoulder to lean on and my partner in crime,
I thank God every day that you are my sibling.*

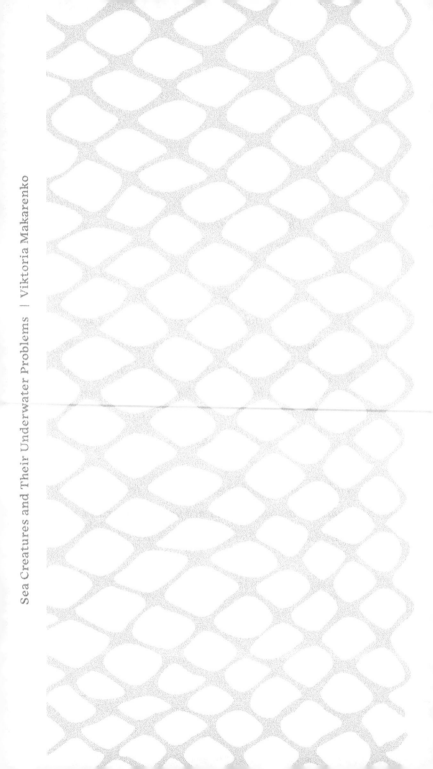

"My marine ecosystem is changing rapidly every single day! Overfishing is corrupting, and ocean acidification is a consistent factor!" the starfish exclaims.

I tell it, "Starfish, I was born to be happy, I was born to be content. But the trials of everyday feel unbearable and have slowly chipped away at every valuable quality I hold dear to myself. I am walking anguish. I am in desperation to be loved, to be held, to be treasured for who I am. I am exhausted of handing my heart to people on a silver platter with a fork and a knife. They rip my flesh in ignorance, they bathe themselves in my tears. Every day I wake up and hate the fact that I woke up as me, I miss all the boys I've loved, I am constantly angry that substance has played such a big role in my life. I want to

believe I am made for more than this! I want to live out all the dreams my mother had before she had me, I want to feel feminine and strong, I want to be a writer, I want to be myself with no guilt, I want to love, I want to live, I want to reach limits beyond my hopes, I want to breath below the sea."

The starfish replies "Sharks get killed all the time just for being themselves, and even then, they love who they are. Everyone in the world wishes for more. I wish I could run through a rainforest and eat a burger. I wish I could fall in love and communicate it with words. You humans are blinded, we are the same. Just because I'm a sea creature, and I don't get the privilege to be on land, doesn't mean I don't have problems under water."

I just ate a jalapeno not knowing it was a jalapeno.

My mouth is on fire.

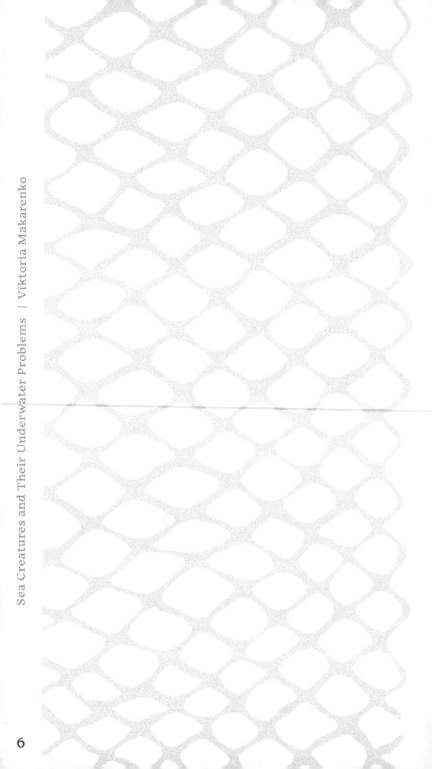

Is part of femininity losing your hairbrush?

Performing a personality you don't own,
to men at the bar?

Yearning for your father's approval?

Biting your nails?

I will outdo your love for me every time.
I want to keep your teeth in a pouch and
carry them with me everywhere I go. I will
take a bite at one when I am out of gum.

You grew up wearing your heart on your sleeve seeking the rubber stamp of others. The world thought your emotions were too big, so you began to ask the world how small it wanted you to be. "For I am the dead grass, I am the unhinged darkness inside all of us that we constantly try to fill using street drugs and naked women. I am the broken nutcracker on Christmas, I am empty so that I can be human first!" You yell this but nobody hears because the rubber stamp does not exist, the approval of others is a mindless reality that you have created for yourself because your father stopped tucking you in and kissing you goodnight when you were 11 years old

A step by step on making your own religion:

- Break yourself open and hold closely to the disapproval of others
- Accept that you lack the meaning of life because your friends disliked the shirt you wore yesterday
- Strictly drink celery juice for a week to cleanse yourself of self-hatred
- Tell everyone you are God

Take my ribs away from me, give them back
to him. Eat the meat of the bones and smile.
Take the fruit, it is not good. It is rotten.
My God, my God I am tired of being
punished for his sins.

As a woman I am told that running towards a dream I will never be able to grasp is my destiny

My emotions swallow me whole; I lose eyesight and walk blindly towards what I want. I am heavy with the urge to reach.

I am heavy because being light means I would have to break it all down and rebuild.

I am six years old. I fall on the playground and my knees are torn up. When it heals, the scarring looks odd. I scratch at it because it looks better with the wound open

There is no sanctuary in the home you created for us. There is only overused conversation and silence when my purpose doesn't serve you.

I dyed my hair blonde today. Nobody hugs me like you did. Nobody suffocates me like you do

I am a supernatural invasive species living
in unfamiliar circumstances, I am tearing
the barrier between Pluto and Mars. I create
a new universe using my neon green hands,
because what becomes of me is so much
greater than space. I thought of this poem
while getting ready this morning.

You'd be surprised to know that aliens do
their eyebrows too

Everyone's afraid of the ocean in fear that they might catch a glimpse of themselves.

You carefully plant avocado seeds in a plastic bowl. Digging your nails into the dirt, you drown it in water. You place the avocado seed under the light. You forget to water it for the next 2 weeks, then 3. You come back to seeing it as a lost cause. You continue your day pretending the avocado seed was something you never cared for.

I grieve the scarcity of dear to heart communion in the relationship I hold with God, for it is hard to thank him for what he has taken away from me. Grief taught me inhumane things, and I am devoted to it. God doesn't care if I'm guilty, so I am guilty always. I captivate that my suffering can become religious.

I give you a band-aid for your papercut right
after you cut my arm off

Please make my entire existences purpose to tenaciously put myself in a situation where no matter what the outcome is I always allow myself to sink into a deeper thought of undying love for you that fills a tremendous void of inconsistency and lack thereof in my life so that I can physically shed my skin off and bend my morals just enough for you to love me back

With messy hair you greet your dad when he comes
home from work. You smell like soil; you've been
outside all day pretending to feed the fairies
Your mother cooks pancakes for dinner
You feel nothing but transports of delight
You don't know the time and your shirt is wrinkled
The warm sun accents your skin through the
transparent windows
You hold your favorite stuffed animal in your left
hand in fear it'll be gone if you let it go
You're too excited for the next day to fall asleep
You make a friend at school and at 10 years of age
you are promised that you no longer have to eat
lunch alone

I am naked on my bed

I am crying

I am so desperately trying to forget

I am so unbearably sad because of your absence

The devil feels guilt too. He doesn't want to be destructive anymore, but it's all that he knows. When it's nighttime a prayer is quietly whispered at his dinner table.

I sigh in relief because I am so high that I think I forgot what it's like to see you smile before you kissed me.

As I step over what's behind me, the crumbs of my past stick to the soles of my feet.

I cut my legs off and grow new ones.

Today I felt grief and suffering along with
absence from something I didn't own,
something I never had in the first place.

I am homesick for a place I cannot return to

The wilting of flowers turns to blooming
of thorns. Leaves that were torn off piece
by piece, when the sun set is when they
reappeared.

the sun rises you're gone

hiding has begun

the intimacy is torn
the flower does not bloom in the morning
it dissipates
there is no longing for opportunity for more
care for water that makes it grow
it destructs as the rays hit
it longs for the maliciousness of it all

a seeking eye searches the premises of my heart

if they see me for who I really am they'll wish
they never looked at all

My entire life smells like you.
I ran my laundry twice to wash away the scent

I am back but I will not remain
I will unravel like a ball of yarn and melt
into the floor
I will come undone and you will never see
me again

For I have let go of every situation, but I
am somehow stuck at that table still asking
you if you like the grilled cheese you just
took a bite from

What if I am full of despair? What if this is all I am?

Be sick of me leave me tell me you can't stand
looking at me

I haven't been sober in weeks and God sends angels to punish me

I hold you as you cry in my arms,
and you never speak to me again.

He calls me pretty and gentle; he calls me wonderful. I grin knowing I'll show him a world made up of his worst nightmares

Being 15 was a great weight and burden.
If I eat less, I can get rid of the heaviness

Pills please! More pills please! Pills, pills, pills! Hello sir, yes, more pills please!

I am so valuable that money tears itself in half
and opens a new milky way
cha ching!!!!!!!!!!!!!!

The hallucinations you voluntarily chose to
fill yourself with turned you into a monster

Towards the darkened alley my hand is held
I am secured with your voice without glancing
at you because

if I look

I'll see a hollowed out body with a soul eaten
alive by drugs

I am never satisfied because I am a woman! I am a boulder of femininity and power! I am in all fonts the best and worst thing to happen to those around me!

I am grief in human form because you are alive
I must grieve you when you're just a minute
away

I am angry because I am told God hates me
I am told I am not enough
I must turn into a saint
because if I am human
then I am an outcast

The sorrow is never ending because no matter
how open I get no matter how ignorant I
become no matter how much I drink no matter
how much I laugh or cry

no matter what

my past will forever dwell on me

I am a bright blooming flower full of pollen and nectar, the bees love me.

I have a headache and I am bits and pieces of
every boy I've ever loved.
I am consumed with their ache because I took
on what they hated about themselves and
learned to love myself with their baggage

I spent the month of march trying to
make everyone around me feel what you
made me feel

It is 3:27pm
I wrap my arms around me in hopes it feels
like a hug from my 15-year-old self

I carve your name into my neck and wear it like a gold chain

Even though you're not around anymore
to hear my deliberate stories and noisy
complaints, I still imagine telling you them
at the end of the day. In you I found a bed
to sleep on and just because I'm not in that
room anymore doesn't mean I can't come
back for a nap

people say that who we date reflects how much
we value ourselves. In disagreement, I found
myself trying to pull at the difficult parts of
people I loved. I wanted to master their flaws.
I valued myself enough to be put in a situation
where I could be destroyed. I felt strong
enough to fight someone else's battles so they
could appreciate mine

If you find yourself washing dishes, hear my voice in the click of the faucet. Remind yourself every day that fall is a season every year and every year you will remember. One day you will choose to live, and you will fall deeply in love with someone no matter what season it is. You will take care of her, and you will take care of yourself.

But when the air gets crisp and the first leaf falls, you will remember it quietly. Not in love, not in lust, but in quiet contentment that it happened, and it is gone, you will remember the smiles you will grieve the laughs. but you won't be hurt or upset, because you will love someone new because it is a new fall.

Every season is different, but it always comes around again.

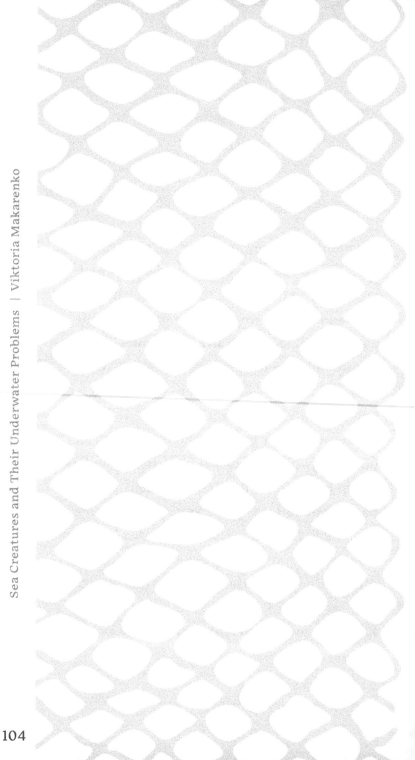

Help me work through it by telling me I was hallucinating, tell me I never mattered, tell me that I took too much melatonin and dreamed a dream that you forget the second you wake up

Before addiction
I was kind
I was soft
I was gentle

I was a new comforter
I was clean sheets

My love for you is worship because I'm
believing you feel the same way without
seeing it happen

You dive deep into me and instead of keeping me afloat you drown me

To love yourself is to eat 2 bowls of soup and ask for one more

Mindlessly say what you're feeling because there will be no outcome if there isn't action taken in the first place!!!!!

I am so eager to move to a different state. I
have daily conversations with myself as to why.
Do I want to give myself permission to flee
from what is haunting me?

Maybe I just want to dye my hair blue again
and call myself a different name

I am so hot, oh my gosh????

I will run through your veins

I will keep you awake at night.
Your miseries will never compare to the
feeling you left me with.

I must rot and you must live with it

What to say when your parents ask you if you're high:

Don't say:
- Yes, I am so sorry.
- Please forgive me it won't happen again.

Try saying this instead:
- NO?? HOW COULD YOU EVEN ASK ME THAT I WOULD NEVER DO THAT I AM SO ANGRY AT YOU HOW COULD YOU JUST ASSUME THAT

The only way to escape reality is to make something else your life style

I need to escape!!! I am a psychotic woman forced to submit to the casualties of the world!!

Stupid stupid sea creatures how could you possibly assume that life on land is any better

When you talk to her, she will be in no way like me
she will be boring
and plain
she will leave you wondering absolutely nothing

You expected me to love with no limits,
from my side and yours

My mother's hands crack with age
she is tired and weary from the day, but she is
so much more than strong and compassionate
she is a raging fire her silence is loud for she is
the epitome of what a woman should be she is
so much more than my mother she is the earth

You are my first real love without a doubt I can say I love you more than I've loved anything else, you make the sun seem dull. I disregard everything else because in you I see everything I've ever wanted.

It is difficult to write when my hands are tied
to every word you said to me

My mother and I have the same eyes, the same nose. the same skin and the same soul. I still complain to her, I am so sick of my face and my stomach and my acne and the way I breath and the way I blink. I hate the way I looked as a child I hate the way I look as a teen. I fear I'll grow up to look the same. I tell her I think I'm disgusting and can't stand to look at myself in the mirror. She says, "you think I'm disgusting too?"

All my experiences are beneath me like a tight rope. If I'm not careful I'll fall to my death

You're pretending to listen
you coax me into feeling validated
you tell me not to worry
but if I truly valued your acceptance of me
as a reason to stay
I'd be long gone.

I roll around in the mud of addiction like a pig

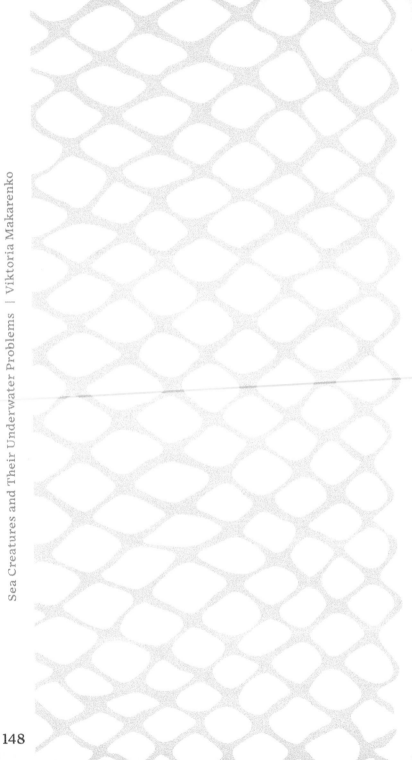

My father tells me, "The reason he's not engaging is not because he's bored. It's because he's overwhelmed with your characteristic strength. He's stupid. You know I hate stupid people."

I'd love to sit down with jellyfish and tell them all about you

I thought that this was what being wanted felt like, I search for what I didn't have enough of

Lay it all out, allow yourself to be devoted to something with no promise. Be vulnerable. Tell them where it hurts and what caused you to bleed out. Stab them back and watch them gasp. Smile and hear them tell you that they are terrified of how eagerly you want others to understand.

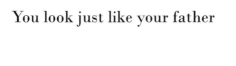

You look just like your father

Daydreaming is a shark because I imagined
you loved me and with 300 pearly whites'
reality bites me

I began to write when I was 15 years old. At the time, I was reading poetry books with simple covers and short poems which encouraged me to write the same. I had always reminded myself that no matter what I wrote, it wouldn't have to be public or shown to anyone, which made it so important to me. It was a healthy way that I could be transparent, that I could say exactly what I wanted to say. No matter how concerning, beautiful, scary, dramatic, kind, hateful it sounded, it was how I felt.

As a woman, it can feel like I must prove my talents before showcasing them. So, if you're a female, and you're reading this, it's not true. Your talents are so important, your dreams are totally conquerable and taking action to do what you love does not require the approval of others. You are strong, emotional, beautiful, and valuable. Don't let anyone tell you otherwise.

Over time writing has opened my heart to understanding that if I can feel such deep emotions as a single human being, then how much more feeling,

ranging from existential dread to pure deliberate happiness, is there in a room of more people. I always have a lot to say, and my emotions tend to lead my life. Therefore, with all my hard work and effort to create this book, I'd like to thank myself for always being vulnerable and never taking that back when people judged me or hurt me. Writing has helped me grow in many ways.

Thank you for reading Sea Creatures and Their Underwater Problems. I hope you feel inclined to unapologetically feel what you feel, and say it out loud, and write about it, after this.

Milton Keynes UK
Ingram Content Group UK Ltd.
UKHW022014310524
443378UK00015B/770